Key Questions

'O' Level Chemistry MCQs

First edition

ISBN 978-1-105-23282-4

Contents

Introduction

This book was written for motivated students with a desire to excel.

This collection of questions follows the latest 'O' Level syllabus closely. It is meant to be used as a guide to aid students in the thorough understanding of 'O' Level Chemistry.

Here's wishing you an enjoyable learning journey.

Please contact me at l.han.07@gmail.com should you have any feedback. It will be very much appreciated. Thank you very much.

1 Collection & Separation Techniques [__ / 30]

1. How can pure water be obtained from a salt solution?
   a. Chromatography
   b. Filtration
   c. Distillation
   d. Crystallization

2. How can sodium chloride be separated from a mixture of sodium chloride and sand?
   a. Add water, filter, crystallize the filtrate
   b. Add water, filter, crystallize the residue
   c. Use a magnet
   d. Heat the mixture and wait for the sand to evaporate away

3. Water and ethanol can be separated by distillation because
   a. They are immiscible liquids
   b. They have different colours
   c. They have different boiling points
   d. They have different densities

4. For two substances to be separated through chromatography, what is necessary?
   a. They must be coloured
   b. They must be soluble in the same solvent
   c. They must have different densities
   d. They must be liquids

5. What happens when a sample of iodine crystals is heated?
   a. A purple gas is evolved
   b. A brown liquid is formed
   c. A purple liquid is formed
   d. A brown gas is evolved

6. Chromatography separates mixtures into their constituents by their different
   a. Colours
   b. Solubilities
   c. Relative molecular masses
   d. Number of valence electrons

7. Copper (II) sulfate crystals should not be obtained by heating to dryness because
    a. The color will change
    b. It will become impure
    c. The crystals will melt into liquid
    d. The crystals will lose their water of crystallization

8. In the fractionating column, there are many small glass beads. Why?
    a. To increase the speed of the separation process
    b. To increase the boiling point of the mixture
    c. To condense the substances that have evaporated
    d. To filter away impurities

9. There are porcelain chips in the fractionating flask. Why?
    a. To increase the speed of the separation process
    b. To get rid of impurities
    c. To ensure a smooth boiling process
    d. To raise the liquid level

10. In fractional distillation of ethanol and water, which is the distillate?
    a. Ethanol, because it has a higher boiling point
    b. Ethanol, because it has a lower boiling point
    c. Water, because it has a higher boiling point
    d. Water, because it has a lower boiling point

11. When two pieces of ice cubes are pressed together, they stick to each other. Why?
    a. Pressure increases the melting point of substances
    b. Pressure decreases the melting point of substances
    c. There are spaces in between the molecules for other molecules to fill up
    d. There is a chemical reaction that binds them together

12. Chromatography is done on colourless solution Substance X to determine if it is pure. What is a potential problem you foresee and what can be done to rectify it?
    a. Individual spots will not be visible. Spray a locating agent.
    b. Individual spots will not be visible. Place under UV light to see.
    c. The mixture cannot be separated. Use another mixture with colour.
    d. The mixture cannot be separated. Use another solvent.

13. Why is crystallization often used as a separation technique in favour over evaporation to dryness?
    a. It is cheaper
    b. It is more accurate
    c. It preserves the water of crystallization
    d. It is faster

14. How do we know when a solution is at its crystallization point?
    a. It changes colour
    b. The solution begins to resemble a crystal rock
    c. It begins to feel hot
    d. Crystals form on a glass rod when it is placed in the solution

15. The graph below shows that any allow of metal A and B

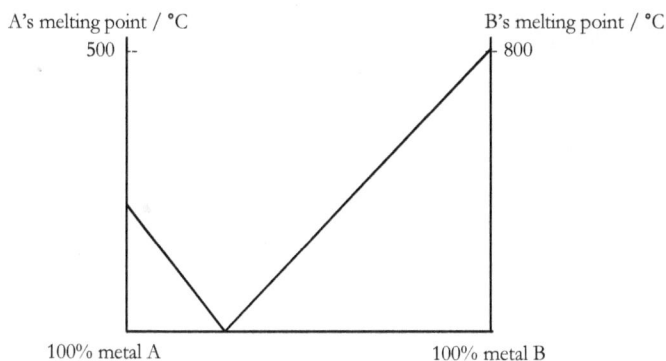

A's melting point / °C
500

B's melting point / °C
800

100% metal A   100% metal B

    a. Must have a melting point higher than that of metal A
    b. Must have a melting point higher than that of metal B
    c. Must have a melting point between than that of metal A and metal B
    d. Must have a melting point higher than that of both metal A and metal B

16. In distillation, what is the function of the condenser?
    a. To lower the temperature so that the distillate can condense
    b. To lower the temperature so that the surrounding impurities can condense
    c. To condense the water vapour in the surrounding air
    d. To condense the mixture when it evaporates

17. A practical use of paper chromatography is not
    a. To identify banned food substances
    b. To investigate the use of drugs in athletes
    c. To separate the components of ink
    d. To separate a solvent from a mixture

18. Which of the following substances is best collected using the following method?

    a. Carbon dioxide
    b. Sulfur dioxide
    c. Helium
    d. Chlorine gas

19. Which property of substance X can conclude that it is a pure substance?
    a. It can conduct electricity in all states
    b. It melts at -5°C
    c. It has a pH of exactly 7.0
    d. It can dissolve in water

20. At what temperature would sugared water be expected to boil?
    a. 100°C
    b. 99°C
    c. 103°C
    d. 0°C

21. Which is the most suitable to measure out 25.6 cm³ of a liquid?
    a. Measuring cylinder
    b. Pipette
    c. Burette
    d. Conical flask

22. A sample of air is passed over anhydrous copper (II) sulfate. No observation is recorded. What can be concluded?
    a. The sample of air is dry
    b. The sample of air is pure
    c. The sample of air is a mixture
    d. The sample of air is not acidic

23. Which of the following does not sublime
    a. Oxygen
    b. Carbon dioxide
    c. Ammonium chloride
    d. Mothballs

24. Aluminium powder is accidentally dropped into a sample of water? How can it be removed?
    a. Simple distillation
    b. Chromatography
    c. Filtration
    d. Fractional distillation

25. What might the R_f value of this spot be?

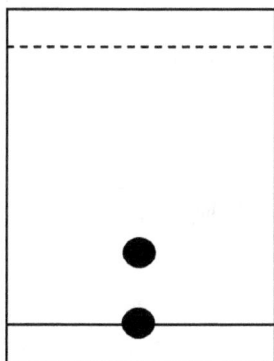

    a. 1.5
    b. 0.5
    c. 0.25
    d. 0.75

26. A sample of ammonium chloride is heated in a test tube. There are two strips of litmus paper at the mouth of the test tube – one blue and one red. Which statement is true after the experiment is complete?
    a. The red litmus paper turns blue and the blue litmus paper turns red
    b. Both litmus paper become blue
    c. Both litmus paper become red
    d. Both litmus paper become white

27. In the same experiment as above, what is observed during the heating process?
    a. The red litmus paper turns blue first
    b. The blue litmus paper turns red first
    c. The litmus papers change colour at the same time
    d. The litmus papers do not change colour

28. A lighted splint is placed in a test tube containing carbon dioxide. What happens?
    a. The lighted splint extinguishes with a pop sound
    b. The lighted splint extinguishes quietly
    c. The lighted splint extinguished, and then is relit
    d. White ppt forms at the bottom of the test tube

29. A sample of gas is bubbled through acidified potassium manganate. The solution turns from purple to colourless. Identify the gas.
    a. Chlorine
    b. Water vapour
    c. Ammonia
    d. Sulfur dioxide

30. Which is the best method of separating two immiscible liquids?
    a. Fractional distillation
    b. Simple distillation
    c. Separating funnel
    d. Filter funnel

2 Atomic Structure [__ / 30]

1. How many neutrons does substance X have?

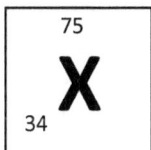

75
X
34

    a. 75
    b. 34
    c. 75-34
    d. 75+34

2. Particle X has an atomic number of 19. Which of the following statements must be true?
    a. It must have 19 neutrons
    b. It must have 19 protons
    c. It must have 19 electrons
    d. The sum of its electrons and protons must add up to 19

3. Which of the following gases would diffuse most rapidly?
    a. NH_3
    b. H_2O
    c. SO_2
    d. N_2

4. What are isotopes?
    a. Atoms of the same element with different number of electrons
    b. Atoms of the same element with different number of neutrons
    c. Elements in the same group in the periodic table
    d. Elements in the same period in the periodic table

5. Which of the following statements need not be true?
    a. An ion must carry a charge
    b. An ion must have 8 valence electrons
    c. An atom must have the same number of protons and electrons
    d. At atom's protons and neutrons contribute to most of its mass

6. Liquid A freezes at a fixed temperature of -200°C. Which other property of A is needed to determine if it is a pure substance?

   a. It boils at 200°C
   b. It is a silvery liquid at room temperature and pressure
   c. It is insoluble in water
   d. It does not react when heated

7. At which position would a white cloud form between the two samples of cotton wool?

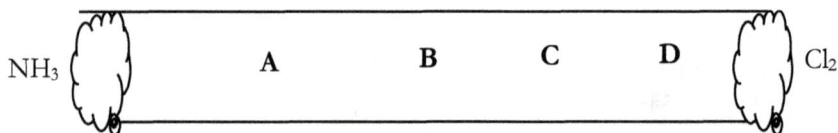

   a. A
   b. B
   c. C
   d. D

8. Which ion has the most shells that contain electrons?

   a. Cl^+
   b. Mg^{2+}
   c. Al^{3+}
   d. Na^+

9. Which pair of substances are isotopes?

   a. H_2O (l) and H_2O (g)
   b. Zn metal and Zn^{2+} ion
   c. Chlorine and bromine
   d. $^{35}_{17}Cl$ and $^{37}_{17}Cl$

10. X is a non-metallic element. Which of the following could be the electronic configuration of X?

   a. 2.8.7
   b. 2.8.2
   c. 2.2.2
   d. 2.2.7

11. Which of the following is a compound?
    a. Air
    b. Copper
    c. Brass
    d. Water

12. Q forms a negative ion with the configuration of 2.8. Identify Q.
    a. Magnesium
    b. Oxygen
    c. Fluorine
    d. Sodium

13. What is the electronic configuration of an oxygen ion?
    a. 2.8.2
    b. 2.8.8
    c. 2.6
    d. 2.8

14. Which atom forms a positive ion of the same configuration as Neon?
    a. Oxygen
    b. Fluorine
    c. Sodium
    d. Copper

15. Which two elements form ions of similar configuration?
    a. Magnesium, Berylium
    b. Magnesium, Oxygen
    c. Neon, Argon
    d. Neon, Sodium

16. Which statement is false?
    a. The lithium ion has 8 valence electrons
    b. The sodium ion has 2 electron shells
    c. Argon is not reactive
    d. Metals form positive ions

17. Given the following information, identify a pair of isotopes

	No. of protons	Atomic mass	No. of electrons
A	15	31	14
B	15	31	15
C	15	31	16
D	17	35	17
E	17	37	17

     a. A and E
     b. A and C
     c. C and D
     d. D and E

18. Using the table above, identify an atom and its positive ion
     a. A and B
     b. A and C
     c. B and C
     d. D and E

19. What is the chemical formula for lithium carbonate?
     a. $Li\,CO$
     b. $Li_2\,CO_3$
     c. $Li\,(CO_3)_2$
     d. $Li\,CO_2$

20. What is the chemical formula for ammonium sulfate?
     a. $NH_4\,SO_4$
     b. $NH_4\,SO_3$
     c. $(NH_4)_2\,SO_4$
     d. $(NH_3)_2\,SO_4$

21. What is the chemical formula for caesium oxide?
     a. $Cs\,O$
     b. $Cs_2\,O$
     c. $Cs\,O_2$
     d. $Cs_2\,O_2$

22. What is the chemical formula for gallium iodide?
    a. Ga I
    b. Ga_2 I
    c. Ga_3 I
    d. Ga I_3

23. What is the chemical formula for radium bromide?
    a. Ra_2 I
    b. Ra I_2
    c. Ra I
    d. Ra_2 I_2

24. Which statement best describes particle X?

	No. of protons	No. of nucleons	No. of electrons
X	5	11	2
Y	6	12	6
Z	7	13	10

    a. It is a metal
    b. It is a non-metal
    c. It is an anion
    d. It is a noble gas

25. Referring to the table in question 24, which of the following statements is true?
    a. X, Y and Z are isotopes as they have the same number of neutrons
    b. X, Y and Z have the same number of electron shells
    c. X, Y and Z have the same number of valence electrons
    d. X, Y and Z have the same number of neutrons but they are not isotopes

26. Referring to the table in question 24, which of the following statements is false?
    a. Particle X is a cation
    b. Particle Y is electrically neutral
    c. Particle Y is a non-metal
    d. Particle Z has more electron shells than particles X and Y

27. The atomic mass of chlorine is 35.5. What does this mean?
    a. An atom of chlorine has 17 protons and 18.5 neutrons
    b. An atom of chlorine has 18.5 protons and 17 neutrons
    c. 35.5 represents the average mass of chlorine isotopes
    d. A chlorine molecule is made of 1 atom with an atomic mass of 35 and 1 atom with an atomic mass of 36

28. Element A is a noble gas. What must be true about it?
    a. It must be a gas
    b. It must have 8 valence electrons
    c. It must conduct electricity
    d. It must form stable compounds

29. What happens when water boils?
    a. It gains electrons
    b. It loses electrons
    c. The number of electrons in the molecule does not change
    d. It is not possible to deduce how the number of electrons change

30. Which is true about an oxygen molecule?
    a. It is made of 2 atoms
    b. It is made of 3 atoms
    c. There is a single bond between the atoms
    d. It is easily broken into atoms

3 Chemical Bonding [__ / 30]

1. Which of the following substances has a macromolecular structure?
   a. Sodium chloride
   b. Water
   c. Silicon dioxide
   d. Sulphur dioxide

2. Which of the following substances has the best electrical conductivity?
   a. H_2O
   b. NaCl
   c. CH_4
   d. Diamond

3. Which of the following substances is likely to have the highest boiling point?
   a. Magnesium sulphate
   b. Nitrogen oxide
   c. Phosphorus dioxide
   d. Fluorine gas

4. If element X forms the ionic compound XBr, how many valence electrons does X have?
   a. 1
   b. 7
   c. 0
   d. 8

5. If element Y forms the covalent compound YCl, how many valence electrons does Y have?
   a. 1
   b. 7
   c. 9
   d. 8

6. With which of the following will sodium form an ionic compound?
   a. Magnesium
   b. Zinc
   c. Iodine
   d. Water

7. Which of the following statements are true about diamond and graphite?
   a. Both conduct electricity although they are covalent compounds
   b. They have van der Waals forces
   c. They are both made of carbon only
   d. They are both made of carbon and lead

8. Why does sodium chloride have a high melting point?
   a. Its structure is that of a tetrahedral, so it has very strong bonds
   b. Strong electrostatic forces hold its ions together
   c. It has very strong van der Waals bonds
   d. It has a sea of electrons

9. Sodium chloride, as it is found at r.t.p., cannot conduct electricity. Why?
   a. The atoms share electrons and so the electrons cannot conduct electricity
   b. There are no free moving electrons in the giant crystal lattice
   c. The sea of electrons are not moving
   d. It is not a metal and only metals can conduct electricity

10. What is true about both graphite and oxygen?
    a. They are both covalent compounds
    b. They can conduct electricity
    c. They have low melting and boiling points
    d. They are macromolecules

11. What is the type of bonding present in iron?
    a. Van der Waals bonding
    b. Metallic bonding
    c. Covalent bonding
    d. Ionic bonding

12. Explain why copper is able to conduct electricity well.
    a. It has mobile ions that conduct electricity
    b. It has mobile electrons that conduct electricity
    c. It is ductile
    d. It is malleable

13. Explain why graphite is a covalent molecule, yet it is able to conduct electricity
    a. It is made of a metallic element
    b. It is magic
    c. It has mobile electons
    d. It has mobile ions

14. Why is carbon dioxide a gas but silicon dioxide a solid at room temperature and pressure?
    a. Carbon dioxide is a simple covalent molecule, silicon dioxide is a giant covalent molecule
    b. Carbon dioxide is a simple covalent molecule, silicon dioxide is a giant ionic crystal
    c. Carbon dioxide is a giant ionic crystal, silicon dioxide is a giant covalent molecule
    d. Carbon dioxide is a giant covalent molecule, silicon dioxide is a simple covalent molecule

15. Why can sodium chloride only conduct electricity in the aqueous and molten states?
    a. The electrons are only mobile in the molten and aqueous states
    b. All liquids are good electrical conductors
    c. The ions are only mobile in the molten and aqueous states
    d. The bonds are too strong in the solid state

16. Why is sulphur dioxide a gas but copper oxide a solid at room temperature and pressure?
    a. Sulfur dioxide is a simple covalent molecule, copper oxide is a giant covalent molecule
    b. Sulfur dioxide is a simple covalent molecule, copper oxide is a giant ionic crystal
    c. Sulfur dioxide is a giant ionic crystal, copper oxide is a giant covalent molecule
    d. Sulfur dioxide is a giant covalent molecule, copper oxide is a simple covalent molecule

17. Which of the following substances has the best electrical conductivity?
    a. H_2O (g)
    b. NaCl (s)
    c. NaCl (aq)
    d. Diamond

18. Which is true about diamond and chlorine?
    a. Both have strong covalent bonds
    b. Both have weak van der waals forces
    c. Both have strong electrostatic forces
    d. Both are made of elements from Group VII of the periodic table

19. Element X has the electronic configuration 2.8.8.6. Which statement is true?
    a. It can only form ionic compounds
    b. It can only form covalent compounds
    c. It can only form ionic or covalent compounds
    d. It can form ionic, covalent or metallic compounds.

20. Why is graphite able to conduct electricity?
    a. It is made of layers
    b. It is made of carbon
    c. It has very strong bonds
    d. It has free moving electrons

21. Which is true about the bonds present in metals?
    a. There are attractive forces between the positive ions and the sea of electrons
    b. There are attractive forces between the electrons in the sea of electrons
    c. There are attractive forces between the positive ions
    d. They break easily

22. What happens when H_2O (l) is boiled?
    a. The ionic bonds heat up until they snap
    b. The van der waals bonds heat up until they snap
    c. The molecules gain kinetic energy and move apart until the bonds between them break
    d. The temperature of the molecules increase gradually to 100^0C

23. Which of the following contains van der Waal's forces?
    a. Calcium chloride
    b. Diamond
    c. Graphite
    d. Copper

24. Substance X conducts electricity in the solid state. Which is likely to be it?
    a. Iodine
    b. Copper (II) chloride
    c. Iron (II) sulphate
    d. Graphite

25. Which is the best description about the bonds in ionic compounds?
    a. Electrostatic attraction between similarly charged ions
    b. Electrostatic attraction between oppositely charged ions
    c. Ionic attraction between electrons and protons
    d. Ionic attraction between electrons and positive ions

26. Which is most true about metallic bonding?
    a. Its strength increases with the charge of the metal ion
    b. Its strength increases with the relative atomic mass of the metal
    c. Its strength decreases with the charge of the metal ion
    d. Its strength decreases with the relative atomic mass of the metal

27. All of the following statements are true except..?
    a. Ionic compounds only conduct electricity when molten or aqueous
    b. All metals conduct electricity
    c. All covalent compounds do not conduct electricity
    d. Ionic compounds have high melting and boiling points

28. Which statement about hydrogen is true?
    a. It forms metallic bonds with metals
    b. It only forms ionic bonds
    c. It only forms covalent bonds
    d. It can form ionic as well as covalent bonds

29. Element X is in group 5. Which is most likely to be true?
    a. It forms a diatomic molecule with 3 shared electrons
    b. It forms a diatomic molecule with 6 shared electrons
    c. It forms an ionic compound with chlorine
    d. It forms an ionic compound with nitrogen

30. Substance X does not conduct electricity in the solid state. Which is substance X?
    a. Graphite
    b. Iron
    c. Copper (II) chloride
    d. Sodium

4 The Mole Concept [__ / 30]

1. When excess carbon monoxide is burnt in 50 cm³ of oxygen gas, what is volume of carbon dioxide produced?
    a. 25 cm³
    b. 50 cm³
    c. 75 cm³
    d. 100 cm³

2. Which statement is true for 1 mole of nitrogen dioxide gas and 1 mole of hydrogen gas?
    a. Both have the same mass
    b. Both have the same number of molecules
    c. Both have the same number of atoms
    d. Both have the same density

3. Which statement is true for 1 mole of HCl (aq) and 1 mole of HCl (g)?
    a. Both have the same volume
    b. Both have the same concentration
    c. Both have the same number of atoms
    d. Both react with magnesium to produce hydrogen gas

4. At room temperate and pressure, what is the ratio of the volume of 2g of hydrogen gas to 32g of oxygen gas?
    a. 1 : 1
    b. 1 : 2
    c. 2 : 1
    d. 1 : 16

5. Which of the following contains the same number of molecules as 10g of hydrogen gas?
    a. 10g of oxygen gas
    b. 60g of carbon
    c. 80g of oxygen gas
    d. 10g of carbon

6. What is the percentage by mass of nitrogen in 20g of ammonium nitrate?
   a. 7.5%
   b. 17.5%
   c. 35%
   d. 37.5%

7. What is the mass of oxygen in 50g of copper (II) oxide?
   a. 5g
   b. 10g
   c. 15g
   d. 20g

8. How many moles of NH_4Cl react with an excess of NaOH to produce 500cm³ of gas?
   a. 50.4
   b. 20.8
   c. 10.4
   d. 15.0

9. What is the volume of sulfuric acid of concentration 2.0 mol/dm³ that is needed to react with excess zinc metal to produce 72cm³ of hydrogen gas?
   a. 1.5 cm³
   b. 15 cm³
   c. 150 cm³
   d. 1500 cm³

10. If 100 cm³ of hydrochloric acid is used to neutralize exactly 250 cm³ of a 1.0 mol/dm³ ammonium hydroxide solution, what is the concentration in g/dm³ of the hydrochloric acid solution used?
    a. 0.07
    b. 0.7
    c. 1.46
    d. 14.6

11. Calculate the mass of water formed at room temperature and pressure when 2 moles of methane combusts in 3 moles of oxygen
    a. 13g
    b. 27g
    c. 54g
    d. 60g

12. Find the amount of gas left over at room temperature and pressure after 24 dm^3 of ethene burns in 24 dm^3 of oxygen
    a. 20 dm^3
    b. 40 dm^3
    c. 60 dm^3
    d. 80 dm^3

13. Find the amount of gas left over immediately after 24 dm^3 of ethene burns in 24 dm^3 of oxygen
    a. 24 dm^3
    b. 48 dm^3
    c. 72 dm^3
    d. 96 dm^3

14. Which of the following has the least number of atoms
    a. 16g of oxygen gas
    b. 40g of magnesium oxide
    c. 2.4 dm^3 of argon gas
    d. 1g of hydrogen gas

15. How many atoms are there in 64g of copper?
    a. 0
    b. 64
    c. 6×10^{23}
    d. 1.2×10^{24}

16. How many atoms are there in 213g of chlorine gas?
    a. 0
    b. 6×10^{23}
    c. 1.2×10^{24}
    d. 1.8×10^{24}

17. How many moles of ions are present in 1.2kg iron (III) sulfate?
    a. 1
    b. 5
    c. 6
    d. 15

18. How many moles of ions are present in 72 dm³ of neon?
    a. 0
    b. 3
    c. 6
    d. 9

19. How many moles of ions are present when 2 moles of $Cu\ SO_4 . 5\ H_2O$ dissolved in water?
    a. 2
    b. 4
    c. 7
    d. 14

20. A hydrocarbon contains 81.82% by carbon and 18.18% by hydrogen. What is its empirical formula?
    a. CH_4
    b. C_2H_5
    c. C_3H_8
    d. C_6H_{12}

21. An organic compound contains 40.0% by mass of carbon and 53.3% by mass of oxygen. What is its empirical formula?
    a. CH
    b. C_2H_5
    c. $C_2H_4O_2$
    d. CHO

22. The relative molecular mass of the compound in the previous question is 60. What is its molecular formula?
    a. CH_4
    b. C_2H_5
    c. CH_3COOH
    d. C_2H_5OH

23. 4g of calcium reacts exactly with 50cm³ of iron (III) chloride solution to form calcium chloride and iron. What is the mass of iron formed?
    a. 1.24g
    b. 2.85g
    c. 3.73g
    d. 4.19g

24. In the experiment above, what is the concentration of iron (III) chloride solution used?
    a. 0.33 mol/dm³
    b. 1.33 mol/dm³
    c. 2.00 mol/dm³
    d. 2.67 mol/dm³

25. In the same experiment above, what is the concentration of calcium chloride formed?
    a. 0.33 mol/dm³
    b. 1.33 mol/dm³
    c. 2.00 mol/dm³
    d. 2.67 mol/dm³

26. The same experiment was repeated with a 1.00 mol/dm³ solution of iron (III) chloride. How will the mass of iron formed change?
    a. Increases by 0.016g
    b. Increases by 0.896g
    c. Decreases by 0.016g
    d. Decreases by 0.896g

27. When 36dm³ of steam is passed across 13.5g of aluminium, the products are aluminium oxide and hydrogen. What is the mass of hydrogen produced?
    a. 0.75g
    b. 1.5g
    c. 18g
    d. 36g

28. What is the mass of leftover reactant in the experiment above?
    a. 13.5g of steam
    b. 18.00g of steam
    c. 4.50g of alumunium
    d. 6.75g of aluminium

29. Nitrogen gas and hydrogen gas react to form ammonia gas as the only product. What is the mass of each gas required to form 12dm³ of ammonia gas?

	Nitrogen gas	Hydrogen gas
a.	3.5g	0.75g
b.	3.5g	1.5g
c.	7g	0.75g
d.	7g	1.5g

30. In the reaction above, which set of gas volumes can produce 18dm³ of ammonia gas?

	Nitrogen gas	Hydrogen gas
a.	0.175 dm³	0.175 dm³
b.	0.375 dm³	0.755 dm³
c.	0.500 dm³	1.000 dm³
d.	0.750 dm³	1.125 dm³

5 Energy Changes [__ / 25]

1. Which of the following reactions are exothermic?
   a. Melting
   b. Boiling
   c. Freezing
   d. Evaporating

2. Which of the following is true of endothermic reactions?
   a. There is more energy involved in bond breaking than bond forming
   b. There is less energy involved in bond breaking than bond forming
   c. More bonds are broken than formed
   d. Fewer bonds are broken than formed

3. When an acid neutralizes a base, the beaker holding the solution feels warm. Why?
   a. Heat is absorbed from the surrounding to break bonds
   b. Heat is absorbed from the surrounding to form bonds
   c. Heat is given out to the surrounding by breaking bonds
   d. Heat is given out to the surrounding by forming bonds

4. In experiment X, an endothermic reaction takes place. Which of the following could be observed?
   a. Bubbles
   b. White ppt
   c. The temperature of the mixture drops
   d. There is strong smell evolved

5. How does a catalyst work?
   a. It lowers the reaction's activation energy
   b. It creates a new pathway with a lower activation energy
   c. In increases the amount of product that can be formed
   d. It eliminates the need to provide heat energy in order for a reaction to take place

6. Which of the following statements is true about a catalyst?
   a. It always increases the enthalpy change of a reaction
   b. It always decreases the enthalpy change of a reaction
   c. It does not change the enthalpy change of a reaction
   d. It can either increase or decrease the enthalpy change of a reaction

7. The enthalpy change of a reaction depends on
   a. The number of bonds formed and broken
   b. The amount of energy needed to form and break bonds
   c. The surrounding temperature
   d. The presence of a catalyst

8. Which statement is not false?
   a. If the products are more stable than the reactants, the reaction is exothermic
   b. If the products are more stable than the reactants, the reaction is endothermic
   c. The reactants and products must have the same level of stability regardless of whether the reaction is exothermic or endothermic
   d. Supplying heat will increase the stability of the products but not the stability of the reactants

9. When a excess of solid X is added to the aqueous solution YZ_2, the products are precipitates of XZ_3 and Y. Given the following information about the bond energies, calculate the total energy change that takes place when 1 mol of X is added to an excess of YZ_2

	kJ/mol
Y-Z	500
X-Z	600

   a. -800 J
   b. - 300 J
   c. +300 J
   d. +800 J

10. A energy profile diagram for this reaction in question 9 looks like..

a.

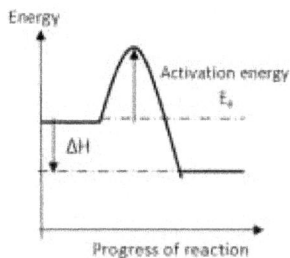

c.

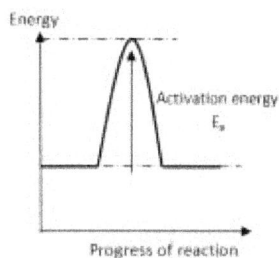

b.

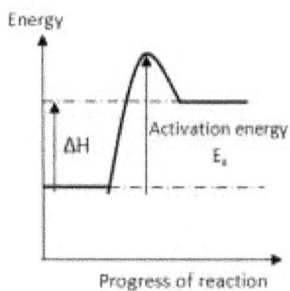

d.

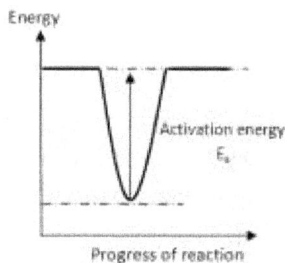

11. For the same reaction as above, suggest one possible way to lower the activation energy of the reaction
    a. Decrease temperature
    b. Decrease concentration of reactants
    c. Add a catalyst
    d. Decrease pressure

12. A sample of methanol (CH_4) combusts completely in oxygen to produce steam and 18dm³ of carbon dioxide gas. The energy produced is found to be 5 kJ. What is the bond energy of a C-H bond?
    a. 0.947 J/mol
    b. 1.667 J/mol
    c. 974 J/mol
    d. 1667 J/mol

13. According to the information given, which compound has the most exothermic combustion reaction

Compound	ΔH of combustion (kJ/mol)
A	- 2000
B	- 2500
C	- 500

   a. A
   b. B
   c. C
   d. They are all equally exothermic

14. Combustion reactions can never be endothermic. Do you agree?
   a. Agree, because heat is always given out
   b. Disagree, because heat can be taken in sometimes
   c. Agree, because all reactions conducted at or above room temperature must be exothermic
   d. Disagree, because if the energy given out when forming bonds is less than the energy taken in to break bonds, the reaction can be endothermic

15. Which statement is false?
   a. Combustion is exothermic and decomposition is endothermic
   b. Both respiration and evaporation are endothermic
   c. Melting is endothermic and freezing exothermic
   d. Neutralization is exothermic and rusting is endothermic

16. A reaction can be said to be exothermic if
   a. More bonds are broken than formed
   b. More bonds are formed than broken
   c. Heat is given out
   d. Heat is taken in

17. What can be deduced about this reaction?

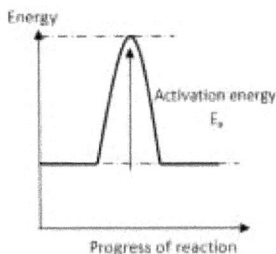

Energy

Activation energy
E_a

Progress of reaction

   a. The number of bonds formed is the same as the number of bonds broken
   b. The energy used in bond forming is the same as the energy used in bond breaking
   c. The energy used in bond breaking is the same as the energy given out in bond forming
   d. The energy absorbed in bond breaking is the same as the energy absorbed in bond forming

18. The bond energy of oxygen molecules is larger than the bond energy of hydrogen molecules because
   a. The H-H bonds require less energy to overcome as hydrogen atoms are smaller than oxygen atoms
   b. The O-O bonds require more energy to overcome as the covalent bonds have more shared electrons
   c. The H=H bonds require less energy to overcome as the covalent bonds have fewer shared electrons
   d. The O=O bonds require more energy to overcome as the covalent bonds have more shared electrons

19. After a reaction, the test tube feels cold. Pick out the false statement.
   a. The reaction is exothermic as the reactants have lost energy
   b. The reaction is endothermic as the reactants have absorbed energy
   c. It cannot be deduced that the activation energy is very low
   d. It cannot be deduced that a catalyst was used

20. Which is the correct graph showing ammonium nitrate being added to water?

a.

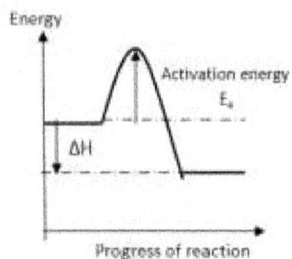

c.

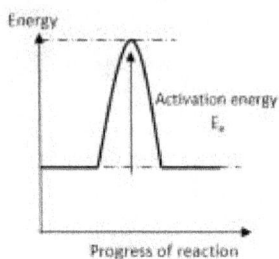

b.

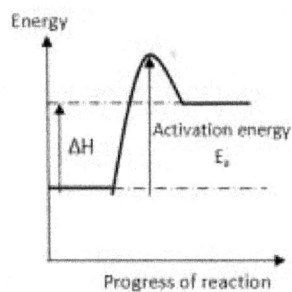

d.

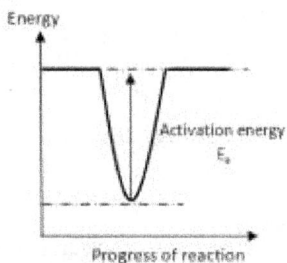

21. Which will produce the most amount of energy?

	Relative molecular mass	ΔH in J/mol
Fuel A	100	+1880
Fuel B	150	+4789
Fuel C	180	- 2146
Fuel D	200	-5987

    a.   500g of fuel A
    b.   200g of fuel B
    c.   300g of fuel C
    d.   150g of fuel D

22. Which of the following temperature-time graphs most accurately depict an endothermic reaction?

a.

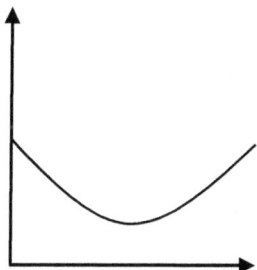

c.

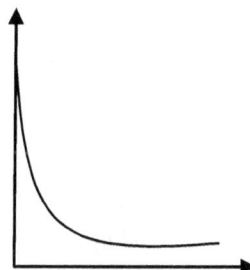

b.

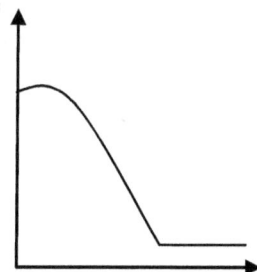

d.

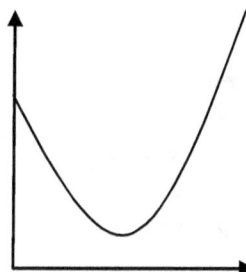

23. What does bond energy mean?
   a. The energy needed to break a single bond between two atoms
   b. The energy needed to break a bond between two atoms
   c. The energy needed to break a bond between 1 mole of atoms
   d. The energy needed to break a bond between 2 moles of atoms

24. Given the following information, calculate the enthalpy change when calcium oxide is added to hydrochloric acid to form calcium chloride and water.

Bond	Bond energy in kJ/mol
Ca – O	1.56
H – O	0.84
Ca – Cl	0.33
H – Cl	1.20

    a.   + 1620 J/mol
    b. +1590 J /mol
    c.   – 1620 J/mol
    d. – 1590 J /mol

25. Using information from the table given above, how much energy is absorbed/released when excess calcium oxide is added to 60 cm³ of 2 mol/dm³ of hydrochloric acid?

    a. 18 J
    b. 50 J
    c. 194 J
    d. 200 J

6 Rate of Reaction [___ / 20]

1. With which of the following solutions of sulphuric acid does copper (II) oxide react with the fastest initial rate of reaction?
    e. 50g of sulphuric acid in 200cm^3 of water
    f. 100g of sulphuric acid in 150cm^3 of water
    g. 150g of sulphuric acid in 100cm^3 of water
    h. 200g of sulphuric acid in 50cm^3 of water

2. Calcium carbonate is reacted with excess aqueous hydrochloric acid to liberate carbon dioxide gas. How can the experiment be changed to liberate twice the amount of carbon dioxide gas?
    a. Use more calcium carbonate
    b. Use more hydrochloric acid
    c. Heat the mixture using a bunsen burner
    d. Increase the concentration of the hydrochloric acid solution

3. Nitrogen gas reacts with hydrogen gas to form ammonia gas. Which change will not affect the rate of this reaction?
    a. Increase temperature
    b. Decrease pressure
    c. Add universal indicator
    d. Add a catalyst

4. Potassium reacts with cold water to form potassium hydroxide and water. Which change will not affect the speed of the reaction?
    a. Increase pressure
    b. Decrease temperature
    c. Add a suitable catalyst
    d. Grind the strip of potassium into powder

5. What can be done to the reaction above to increase the concentration of potassium hydroxide?
    a. Increase pressure
    b. Decrease pressure
    c. Use less potassium
    d. Evaporate away some of the water

6. When iron is added to nitric acid, hydrogen is formed. The solid line shows how the volume of gas collected varies with time. In which diagram does the dotted line show the new pattern when the iron block is ground into powder?

a.

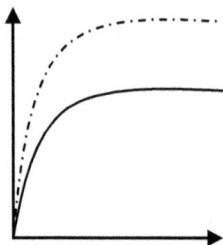

c.

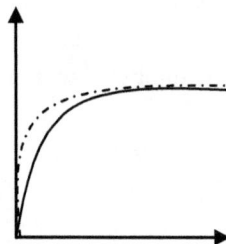

b.

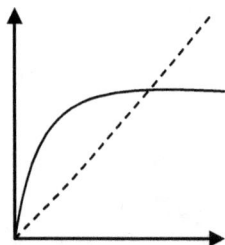

d.

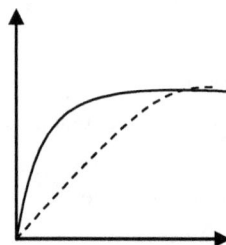

7. What can be done to increase the volume of gas collected when excess zinc carbonate chips are added to sulfuric acid?
   a. Increase the pressure
   b. Grind the chips into powder
   c. Increase the concentration of the acid
   d. Increase the temperature

8. In the same reaction above, what would happen if the mass of zinc carbonate added is doubled?
   a. The volume of gas collected is doubled
   b. The volume of gas collected is halved
   c. The concentration of zinc sulfate doubles
   d. The concentration of zinc sulfate remains the same

9. 23g of sodium is added to 1dm^3 of 1 mol/dm^3 sulfuric acid. What happens when the concentration of the acid is doubled?

	Speed of reaction	Volume of gas collected
a.	Increases	No change
b.	Decreases	Increases
c.	Increases	No change
d.	No change	Increases

10. Which statement is true?
   a. Pressure only affects the rate of reaction if a reactant is in the gaseous state
   b. Pressure only affects the rate of reaction if a product is in the gaseous state
   c. Pressure only affects the rate of reaction if both the reactants and the products are in the gaseous state
   d. Pressure will affect the rate of reaction of any reaction regardless of the states of the reactants or products

11. Which statement is not true?
   a. The concentration of a solution will always affect the rate of reaction, even if it is not the limiting reactant
   b. Powder has a larger surface area than lumps of the same mass
   c. Pressure increases the rate of effective collisions by forcing the particles closer to each other
   d. Pressure increases the rate of effective collisions by increasing the number of particles involved in the reaction

12. Which does not explain why an increase in temperature increases rate of reaction?
   a. It causes the size of the particles to increase, which increases the chances of effective collision
   b. It causes the particles to move faster
   c. It causes the particles to gain kinetic energy
   d. It causes the particles to bump into each other more frequently

13. The entire reaction shown below took 10 minutes. How long did it take for half the reaction?

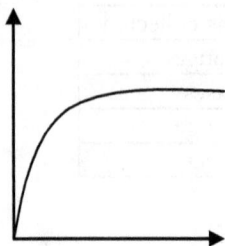

    a.   2.5 minutes
    b.   5 minutes
    c.   7.5 minutes
    d.   9 minutes

14. Magnesium was added to a volume of nitric acid on a weighing scale. Which line shows the graph of mass versus time?

a.

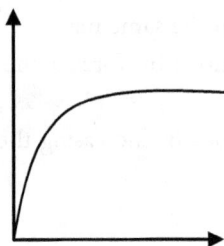

c.

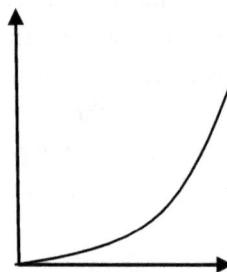

b.

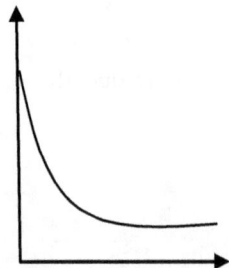

d.

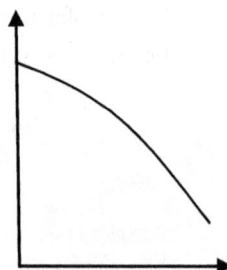

15. The solid line is reaction 1. The dotted line is when the reaction is repeated. Which statement is most accurate?

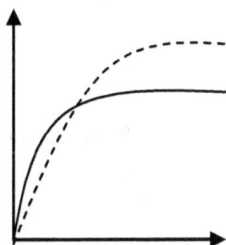

    a.   Only the temperature has increased

    b.   Only the concentration of the limiting reactant has increased

    c.   The temperature has increased and the amount of the reactant in excess has also increased

    d.   A catalyst was added

16. What could have happened to change the solid line to the dotted line in the reaction between hydrochloric acid and excess zinc chips?

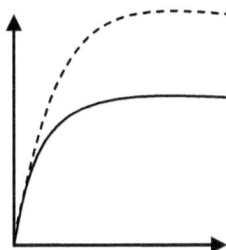

    a.   Powdered zinc was used instead

    b.   Sulfuric acid was used instead

    c.   More zinc chips were added

    d.   The temperature was raised

17. Hydrogen peroxide decomposes to form water and oxygen. Which would not increase the volume of oxygen formed?

    a.   Increasing the concentration of hydrogen peroxide

    b.   Increasing the volume of hydrogen peroxide

    c.   Increasing the temperature of the hydrogen peroxide

    d.   Increasing the mass of hydrogen peroxide

18. Adding a catalyst to the decomposition of hydrogen peroxide
    a. Shorten the time taken to collect the maximum volume of oxygen
    b. Increase the amount of oxygen collected
    c. Increase the amount of water collected
    d. Decrease the amount of hydrogen peroxide decomposed

19. 10g of magnesium carbonate chips was added to an excess volume of acid. If 20g of powder had been used instead, what would not have happened?
    a. More carbon dioxide collected
    b. Increased rate of reaction
    c. More acid neutralized
    d. More salt formed

20. If the concentration of acid were increased instead of the mass of magnesium chips, how would the reaction be affected?
    a. More carbon dioxide collected
    b. Increased rate of reaction
    c. More acid neutralized
    d. More salt formed

7 Redox reactions [__ / 30]

1. When a metal atom becomes an ion,
   a. It is oxidized
   b. It is reduced
   c. It is neither oxidized nor reduced
   d. There is a redox reaction taking place

2. When a non-metal atom becomes an ion,
   a. It gains electrons and is reduced
   b. It gains electrons and is oxidized
   c. It gains protons and is reduced
   d. It gains electrons and is oxidized

3. A gas is passed over heated copper (II) oxide. Copper and steam are produced. Identify the gas.
   a. Oxygen
   b. Hydrogen
   c. Carbon dioxide
   d. Steam

4. Which is true about a reducing agent?
   a. It reduces others by oxidizing itself
   b. It oxidizes others by reducing itself
   c. It reduces others but is not necessarily oxidized or reduced
   d. It oxidizes others but is not necessarily oxidized or reduced

5. When a reducing agent is added to acidified potassium dichromate (VI), the solution changes from orange to green because…?
   a. The reducing agent has been oxidized
   b. The reducing agent has been reduced
   c. The acidified potassium dichromate (VI) has been oxidized
   d. The acidified potassium dichromate (VI) has been reduced

6. Potassium dichromate and potassium manganate are both oxidizing agents because...?
    a. They both contain potassium
    b. They both contain transition metals
    c. They are both colored
    d. They oxidize other substances and are themselves reduced

7. Which is true about all oxidizing and reducing agents?
    a. They must be coloured
    b. They must contain a transition element
    c. All chemical reactions involving them must be redox reactions
    d. All reactions involving them must give out effervescence

8. All of the following are redox reactions except
    a. Boiling
    b. Displacement
    c. Forming carbon monoxide from carbon dioxide
    d. Extraction iron from haematite

9. A reducing agent is added to a purple solution X. The solution loses its colour. Identify this solution X.
    a. Universal indicator
    b. Phenolphthalein
    c. Acidified potassium dichromate (VI)
    d. Acidified potassium manganate (VII)

10. When a piece of magnesium strip is dropped into a beaker of sulfuric acid, a salt is formed and hydrogen gas is released. Choose the correct statement.
    a. Magnesium is the oxidizing agent because it has been oxidized
    b. Sulfuric acid is the reducing agent because it has been reduced
    c. Magnesium is the reducing agent because it has been oxidized
    d. Hydrogen gas is the oxidizing agent because it has been reduced

11. In the experiment above, what happens to the oxidation state of magnesium?
    a. Increases from -2 to 0
    b. Increases from 0 to +2
    c. Decreases from +2 to 0
    d. Decreases from 0 to -2

12. Hydrogen peroxide (H_2O_2) reacts with silver oxide to produce silver deposits, water and oxygen gas. Which statement does not represent this reaction?
    a. Silver is oxidized from an oxidation state of +1 to 0
    b. Silver is oxidized from an oxidation state of 0 to +1
    c. Silver is reduced from an oxidation state of +1 to 0
    d. Silver is reduced from an oxidation state of 0 to +1

13. What is the role of hydrogen peroxide in the experiment above?
    a. To oxidize silver and reduce oxygen
    b. To oxidize oxygen and reduce silver
    c. To oxidize both silver and oxygen
    d. To reduce both silver and oxygen

14. When iron is manufactured from haematite, iron (III) oxide reacts with carbon monoxide to produce iron and carbon dioxide. Is this a redox reaction?
    a. Yes, Fe_2O_3 is the reducing agent and CO is the oxidizing agent
    b. Yes, Fe_2O_3 has been reduced and CO has been oxidized
    c. No, because there is no change in oxidation state
    d. No, because there is no colour change

15. Which is true about hydrogen peroxide?
    a. It is an oxidizing agent only
    b. It is a reducing agent only
    c. It is both an oxidizing as well as reducing agent
    d. It is neither an oxidizing nor reducing agent

16. When a metal is reacted with an acid,
    a. The metal is reduced
    b. The acid is oxidized
    c. The metal acts as a reducing agent
    d. The metal acts as an oxidizing agent

17. What happens when iron rusts?
    a. It is oxidized by gaining electrons
    b. It is reduced by gaining electrons
    c. It is oxidized by losing electrons
    d. It is reduced by losing electrons

18. Chlorine gas is bubbled through aqueous potassium iodide. What happens?
    a. The potassium iodide solution turns brown as it has been oxidized
    b. The potassium iodide solution turns brown as it has been reduced
    c. The potassium iodide solution decolorizes as it has been oxidized
    d. The potassium iodide solution decolorizes as it has been reduced

19. What does the (VII) in acidified potassium manganate (VII) mean?
    a. The compound has 7 valance electrons
    b. The oxidation state of the compound is +7
    c. The oxidation state of the compound is -7
    d. The oxidation state of the manganate ion in the compound is +7

20. Which of the following reactions are redox reactions?

Reaction 1	Neutralization
Reaction 2	Displacement
Reaction 3	Extraction of iron from haematite

    a. Reaction 2 only

    b. Reactions 1 and 2 only

    c. Reactions 1 and 3 only

    d. Reactions 1, 2 and 3

21. The oxidation state of sulphur in a sulphate ion is

    a. $+6$

    b. $+8$

    c. -6

    d. -8

22. Chlorine gas is bubbled through acidified potassium manganate (VII). What happens?

    a. No visible change is observed

    b. The chlorine gas causes the solution to turn yellowish green

    c. The potassium manganate solution turns purple as it has been reduced

    d. The potassium manganate solution decolorizes as it has been reduced

23. Regarding the reaction in which carbon monoxide is formed from carbon dioxide, all of the following statements are false, except for one. Which is it? [1]

    a. Carbon monoxide is oxidized

    b. Carbon is reduced

    c. Carbon dioxide is oxidized

    d. It is a redox reaction

24. The oxidation states of chromium and manganese in the oxidizing agents potassium dichromate and potassium manganite differ by
    a. 0
    b. 1
    c. 2
    d. 3

25. When copper metal is added to hydrochloric acid, what happens?
    a. Only copper is oxidized
    b. Only hydrochloric acid is oxidized
    c. Both copper and hydrochloric acid are oxidized
    d. None of the substances are oxidized

26. With which of the following substances will aqueous iron (II) sulphate have a redox reaction with?
    a. Aqueous potassium iodide
    b. Copper metal
    c. Aqueous sodium sulphate
    d. Acidified potassium manganate (VII)

27. What happens to chlorine in the reaction shown below?

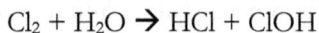

$$Cl_2 + H_2O \rightarrow HCl + ClOH$$

    a. It has been oxidized only
    b. It has been reduced only
    c. It has been oxidized as well as reduced
    d. It has been neither oxidized nor reduced

28. Calculate the oxidation state of the underlined elements in K$\underline{Mn}$O$_4$ and K$_2$$\underline{Cr_2}O_7$
    a. +3 and +6 respectively
    b. +5 and +3 respectively
    c. +1 and +2 respectively
    d. +5 and +6 respectively

29. Calculate the oxidation state of the underlined elements in $\underline{C}O_2$ and $\underline{C}O$
    a. +4 and +6 respectively
    b. +2 and +4 respectively
    c. +4 and +2 respectively
    d. +2 and +1 respectively

30. Calculate the oxidation state of the underlined elements in $\underline{N}H_3,$ $\underline{N}H_4OH$ and $\underline{N}O_2$
    a. +3, +5 and +6 respectively
    b. +5, +3 and +2 respectively
    c. -3, -3 and +4 respectively
    d. +3, -3 and +4 respectively

8 Acids, Bases, Salts [__ / 30]

1. Element X burns in air to form an oxide that dissolves in both acids and alkalis. What is X likely to be?
   a. Carbon
   b. Potassium
   c. Zinc
   d. Calcium

2. Bubbles are seen when which of the following is added to dilute sulfuric acid?
   a. NaOH (aq)
   b. Cu (s)
   c. MgO
   d. $ZnCO_3$

3. Which of the following is true of alkalis in aqueous solutions?
   a. They produce CO_2 (g) when reacted with metal carbonates
   b. They produce a pungent gas when reacted with ammonium salts
   c. They produce bubbles when neutralized with acids
   d. They turn blue litmus paper red

4. When Y dissolves in HNO_3 (aq), the gas produced extinguished a lighted splint with a 'pop' sound. What could Y be?
   a. Hydrogen gas
   b. Carbon dioxide
   c. Zinc
   d. Copper

5. When $CaCo_3$ is added to aqueous HCl, which of the following takes place?
   a. A gas is produced that turns limewater chalky
   b. There is a white ppt produced
   c. A gas is liberated that relights a glowing splint
   d. The resulting solution turns red litmus paper blue

6. Which compound will not neutralize acidic soils?
   a. Sodium carbonate
   b. Sodium chloride
   c. Sodium oxide
   d. Sodium hydroxide

7. A sample of aqueous nitric acid has a pH value of 2. What could be a possible pH value after adding Potassium Iodide?
   a. 2
   b. 5
   c. 7
   d. 9

8. When Ammonium Chloride is added to solution P, gas Q is liberated. Which is likely to be P and Q?

	P	Q
a.	Hydrochloric acid	Chlorine
b.	Calcium hydroxide	Carbon dioxide
c.	Potassium hydroxide	Ammonia
d.	Water	Ammonia

9. Which of the following will produce Copper(II) Sulphate when added to H_2SO_4?
   I. Copper   II. Copper Oxide
   III. Copper Carbonate   IV. Copper Hydroxide

   a. I only
   b. II and III only
   c. II, III and IV only
   d. All of the above

10. Which of the following react to produce salt and water *only*?
    a. HCl and $Ca(OH)_2$
    b. H_2SO_4 and $MgCl_2$
    c. $Ca(OH)_2$ and NH_4Cl
    d. HCl and $ZnCO_3$

11. Barium carbonate is added to an excess of nitric acid. What is observed?
    a. Effervescence
    b. White ppt
    c. Yellow ppt
    d. An explosion

12. What happens in the reaction between calcium hydroxide and ammonium sulphate?
    a. Gas produced turns blue litmus paper red
    b. Gas produced turns red litmus paper blue
    c. Gas produced relights a glowing splint
    d. Gas produced pops a lighted splint with a 'pop' sound

13. What happens in the reaction between hydrochloric acid and copper?
    a. Hydrogen gas is produced
    b. A white ppt is formed
    c. There is no reaction
    d. A pink deposit is formed

14. What happens in the reaction between sulfuric acid and iron (III) carbonate?
    a. Solution turns from green to brown
    b. Solution turns from colourless to blue
    c. Effervescence is observed
    d. A reddish brown ppt is formed

15. What happens in the reaction between phosphoric acid and aluminium oxide?
    a. Nothing happens
    b. A white ppl forms
    c. There is a gas produced
    d. Water forms

16. A river is too acidic. What should be done?
    a. Add calcium oxide
    b. Add sodium hydroxide
    c. Add sodium chloride
    d. Add calcium chloride

17. Which reaction does not take place?
    a. NaOH and H_2SO_4
    b. H_2SO_4 and $BaCO_3$
    c. HCl and $MgCO_3$
    d. CuO and HNO_3

18. How can sulfuric acid be distinguished from hydrochloric acid?
    a. Add barium nitrate
    b. Add sodium chloride
    c. Add limewater
    d. Use litmus paper

19. Substance X forms a white ppt with silver nitrate. It also forms a white ppt with aqueous ammonia that dissolves in excess. Identify substance X.
    a. Lead (II) sulfate
    b. Lead (II) chloride
    c. Zinc sulfate
    d. Zinc chloride

20. Substance Z gives off a gas that turns red litmus paper blue when aluminium powder is added. It also produces a blue ppt when NaOH is added. What is Z?
    a. Copper (II) nitrate
    b. Copper (II) hydroxide
    c. Ammonium nitrate
    d. Ammonium hydroxide

21. Which is the most suitable method of preparing calcium sulfate crystals?
    a. Titration
    b. Precipitation
    c. Add excess base
    d. Oxidation

22. 100 cm^3 of 1 mol/dm^3 nitric acid is added to 100 cm^3 of 1 mol/dm^3 calcium hydroxide. Universal indicator is added. What is the colour of the solution?
    a. Green
    b. Yellow
    c. Red
    d. Purple

23. All acids must
    a. Fully dissociate to form H^+ ions
    b. Be soluble
    c. React with copper
    d. Have OH^- ions

24. Which salt is most suitably prepared using titration?
    a. Iron (II) hydroxide
    b. Silver chloride
    c. Potassium nitrate
    d. Zinc chloride

25. What is the difference between a strong alkali and a weak alkali?
    a. The concentration of H^+ ions
    b. The concentration of OH^- ions
    c. The color
    d. Weak alkalis are organic, strong alkalis are not

26. What should be added to nitric acid to prepare copper (II) nitrate?
    a. Copper metal
    b. Copper (II) carbonate
    c. Copper (II) chloride
    d. Copper (II) sulfate

27. All alkalis
    a. Can conduct electricity
    b. Turn blue litmus paper red
    c. Turn universal indicator yellow
    d. Are insoluble

28. Which ionic equation represents neutralization
    a. $HNO_3 + NaOH \rightarrow NaNO_3 + H_2O$
    b. $H^+ + OH^- \rightarrow H_2O$
    c. $Ag^+ + Cl^- \rightarrow AgCl$
    d. $Fe^{2+} + Cu \rightarrow Fe + Cu^{2+}$

29. When phenolphthalein changes color,
     a. The solution is at pH 7
     b. The solution is acidic
     c. The solution is alkaline
     d. The solution is water

30. 24g of magnesium is added to an excess of 2 mol/dm³ HCl. Find the volume of gas produced.
     a. 12 dm³
     b. 24 dm³
     c. 48 dm³
     d. 0 dm³

9 Periodicity [__ / 50]

1. Element X is in Group VII and Period 5 of the periodic table. Which of the following is true?
    a. It forms an amphoteric oxide
    b. It is a good conductor of electricity in the molten state
    c. It displaces chlorine from an aqueous chloride salt
    d. It is displaced by chlorine from an aqueous chlorine salt

2. Element Y is directly above element Z in Group I of the periodic table. Which is correct?
    a. Y is more reactive than Z
    b. Z is more reactive than Y
    c. They are equally reactive
    d. It is impossible to deduce which is more reactive

3. Which of the following elements exist as diatomic molecules at room r.t.p.?
    a. Neon
    b. Sodium
    c. Zinc
    d. Nitrogen

4. Element P is monotomic and does not form ions. What can be deduced about P?
    a. It is highly reactive
    b. It is in Group I of the periodic table
    c. It is in Group VII of the periodic table
    d. It is highly unreactive

5. Which statement about groups in the periodic table is correct?
    a. Moving down a group, the elements become increasingly metallic
    b. Elements in the same group have the same number of electrons
    c. Elements in the same group have the same level of reactivity
    d. Moving down Group VII, the elements have increasingly higher boiling points

6. What happens when chlorine gas is bubbled into a solution of aqueous potassium bromide?
   a. Brown gas is evolved
   b. Purple gas is evolved
   c. Bromine displaces chlorine
   d. Chlorine displaces potassium

7. Which element is least likely to form an oxide?
   a. Sodium
   b. Zinc
   c. Neon
   d. Chlorine

8. Element X is found directly below potassium in the periodic table. Which of the following must be true?
   a. It readily displaces lithium ions only
   b. It readily displaces caesium ions only
   c. It readily displaces both lithium and caesium ions
   d. It readily displaces neither lithium nor caesium ions

9. Element Y is found directly below element X in group VII of the periodic table. Which of the following must be true?
   a. If X exists as a gas at r.t.p., Y must also exist as a gas
   b. If X exists as a gas at r.t.p., Y must exist as either a gas or a liquid
   c. If X exists as a gas at r.t.p., Y can exist as either a gas, liquid or solid
   d. The state of Y cannot be deduced from the state of X

10. Which of the following is true about the ions of group VII elements?
    a. They must carry a positive charge of 1
    b. They must carry a negative charge of 1
    c. They can carry either a positive or negative charge of 1
    d. They can carry a charge of any size as long as it is negative

11. Chlorine gas is bubbled into a solution of aqueous sodium bromide. What is observed?
   a. Solution turns colourless because bromine is displaced
   b. Solution turns colourless because chlorine is displaced
   c. Solution turns brown because bromine is displaced
   d. Solution turns brown because chlorine is displaced

12. Which balanced ionic equation with state symbols represents the reaction in question 11?
   a. Cl^- (aq) + Br_2 (aq) → Cl_2 (aq) + Br^- (aq)
   b. Cl^- (g) + Br_2 (aq) → Cl_2 (aq) + Br^- (aq)
   c. Cl_2 (aq) + Br^- (aq) → Cl^- (aq) + Br_2 (aq)
   d. Cl_2 (g) + Br^- (aq) → Cl^- (aq) + Br_2 (aq)

13. Which is the type of reaction taking place in question 11?
   a. Neutralization
   b. Displacement
   c. Precipitation
   d. Titration

14. Why do the boiling points for elements in group I decrease down the group?
   a. The number of valence electrons increases
   b. The number of valence electrons decreases
   c. The number of electron shells increases
   d. The number of electron shells decreases

15. Why do the boiling points of elements in group VII increase down the group?
   a. The van der Waals forces between the molecules get stronger
   b. The van der Waals forces between the atoms get stronger
   c. The electrostatic attraction between the molecules get stronger
   d. The attraction between the ions and the sea of electrons get stronger

16. Going down the group, Group I elements become more reactive. Why?
    a. It gets easier to lose the valence electrons
    b. It gets easier to gain electrons
    c. The size gets bigger
    d. The number of electrons increases

17. Group VII elements become less reactive down the group. Why?
    a. It gets easier to lose the valence electrons
    b. It gets easier to gain electrons
    c. The size gets bigger
    d. The number of electrons increases

18. The following information about the elements X, Y and Z are provided.

	Melting point	Boiling point
X	60.0°C	98.7°C
Y	29.7°C	63.3°C
Z	47.8°C	79.9°C

Elements X, Y and Z lie in group VII of the periodic table. Arrange them in order of increasing relative molecular mass.

    e. X, Y, Z
    f. Y, X, Z
    g. Y, Z, X
    h. X, Z, Y

19. Arrange them in order of increasing reactivity.
    a. X, Z, Y
    b. X, Y, Z
    c. Y, Z, X
    d. Y, X, Z

20. Which of the following, when added to a solution of aqueous sodium bromine, will result in a colour change of the solution? [1]
    a. Potassium
    b. Zinc
    c. Chlorine
    d. Neon

21. If elements P and Q are in the same period of the periodic table, they must have the same number of... [1]
    a. Electrons
    b. Valence electrons
    c. Electron shells
    d. Neutrons

22. Element X forms an oxide that neutralizes aqueous sulphuric acid to form a salt and water. This oxide does not react with aqueous calcium hydroxide. Which is most likely to be element X? [1]
    a. Lithium
    b. Zinc
    c. Fluorine
    d. Argon

23. An atom of element A gains an electron to attain the structure of a noble gas. It is the most reactive element in its group. What could element A possibly be? [1]
    a. Lithium
    b. Francium
    c. Fluorine
    d. Astatine

24. Which of the following must increase across a period in the periodic table? [1]
    a. Atomic mass
    b. Charge of ion formed
    c. pH
    d. Boiling point

25. Which of the following must increase down a group in the periodic table? [1]
    a. Atomic mass
    b. pH
    c. Reactivity
    d. Boiling point

26. Which of the following must be true if X displaces Y from an aqueous solution of its ionic salt? [1]
    a. X must be below Y in a group
    b. X must be above Y in a group
    c. X must be more reactive than Y
    d. X must be less reactive than Y

27. Which element is most likely to form an oxide that can neutralize aqueous potassium hydroxide? [1]
    a. Potassium
    b. Chlorine
    c. Hydrogen
    d. Xenon

28. Element A is in the same group as Nitrogen in the periodic table. Which of the following statements is true? [1]
    a. It has 2 electron shells
    b. It has 7 electrons
    c. It has 7 protons
    d. It has 5 valence electrons

29. At r.t.p., iodine is a solid while bromine is a gas. Why is this so? [1]
    a. Iodine molecules are held together by stronger ionic forces
    b. Iodine molecules are held together by stronger electrostatic forces
    c. Iodine molecules are held together by stronger van der waals's forces
    d. Iodine molecules are held together by stronger covalent forces

30. There are three elements A, B and C. They are sodium, iodine and argon. However, they are all mixed up and you do not know which is which. Element A reacts with water to form a soluble compound and an insoluble gas. Identify element A. Explain your choice.
    a. Sodium
    b. Iodine
    c. Argon
    d. Impossible to tell

31. Element B is found in light bulbs. Identify elements B and C.
    a. B is sodium, C is iodine
    b. B is sodium, C is argon
    c. B is argon, C is iodine
    d. B is argon, C is sodium

32. Elements P, Q and R have consecutive proton numbers. Q is inert. Which two elements belong in the same period of the periodic table?
    a. P and Q
    b. Q and R
    c. P and R
    d. All are in the same period

33. Two of the elements react to form a soluble salt that can conduct electricity when in the aqueous state. Which two are they?
    a. P and Q only
    b. Q and R only
    c. P and R only
    d. Any combination is possible

34. Elements W, X, Y and Z have consecutive proton numbers and are found in period 3. How would you expect their electrical conductivities to vary?
    a. Increase
    b. Decrease
    c. Increase, then decrease
    d. Decrease, then increase

35. Which 2 physical properties would be expected in a compound formed from elements W and Z (from the previous question) at room temperature?
    a. Malleable and ductile
    b. Colorless and high melting point
    c. Good electrical conductor and high melting point
    d. Low boiling point and non electrical conductor

36. Which 2 physical properties would be expected in a compound formed from elements Y and Z (from qn 34) at room temperature?
    a. Malleable and ductile
    b. Colorless and high melting point
    c. Good electrical conductor and high melting point
    d. Low boiling point and non electrical conductor

37. What increases across a period?
    a. Ionic charge
    b. Melting point
    c. Electrical conductivity
    d. Atomic number

38. Across a period, what property of the elements increases and then decreases?
    a. Boiling point
    b. pH
    c. Relative atomic mass
    d. Number of electron shells

39. An element forms ions with varying oxidation states. What must be false?
    a. It conducts electricity
    b. It is a reducing agent
    c. It is an oxidizing agent
    d. It has a varying proton number

40. Which of the following must be true if X displaces Y from an aqueous solution of its ionic salt?
    a. X must be below Y in a group
    b. X must be above Y in a group
    c. X must have a lower melting point than Y
    d. X must have a higher melting point than Y

41. Element X is directly above bromine in the periodic table. Which of the following must be true?
    a. It displaces a fluoride ion to form MgX
    b. It displaces a fluoride ion to form MgX_2
    c. It displaces an iodide ion to form KX
    d. It displaces an iodide ion to form KX_2

42. Element Y is found directly below element X in group I of the periodic table. Which of the following is most true?
    a. If X exists as a liquid at r.t.p., Y exists as a solid
    b. If X exists as a liquid at r.t.p., Y exists as either a liquid or a solid
    c. If X exists as a liquid at r.t.p., Y exists as a gas
    d. If X exists as a liquid at r.t.p., Y exists as either a liquid or a gas

43. Element A is in the same period as nitrogen in the periodic table. It loses 2 electrons to form an ionic compound with an anion. Which of the following is true?
    a. A^{2+} has a stable duplet electronic structure
    b. A^{2+} has a stable octet electronic structure
    c. A^{2-} has a stable duplet electronic structure
    d. A^{2-} has a stable octet electronic structure

44. Which, when added to a solution of aqueous bromine, is most likely to decolorize it?
    a. Chlorine gas
    b. Iodine vapour
    c. Sodium chloride
    d. Sodium iodide

45. Which element is most likely to form a carbonate that produces only salt, water and carbon dioxide when added to aqueous hydrochloric acid?
    a. Rubidium
    b. Hydrogen
    c. Chlorine
    d. Xenon

46. A piece of potassium is dropped into a beaker of distilled water containing phenolphthalein. Which is not true?
   a.   Effervescence is seen
   b.   Potassium displaces hydrogen
   c.   There is a redox reaction
   d.   The phenolphthalein turns green

47. Aqueous iron (II) chloride is then added. What happens?
   a.   Green ppt forms
   b.   Reddish brown ppt forms
   c.   The solution turns chalky
   d.   Effervescence is seen

48. A gaseous element X is bubbled into an aqueous solution of potassium bromide. State the color of aqueous potassium bromide.
   a.   Brown
   b.   Pink
   c.   Colourless
   d.   Blue

49. X lies directly above bromine in the periodic table. What is observed when X is bubbled into the solution?
   a.   Solution turns brown
   b.   Brown ppt forms
   c.   Pink deposits are formed
   d.   Effervescence is seen

50. A small piece of sodium is then added to the solution. What is observed?
   a.   Nothing
   b.   Effervescence is seen
   c.   There is a green ppt
   d.   There is a brown ppt

10 Metals [__ / 30]

1. Which of the following is most likely to be a transition metal?

	Melting point	Colour of aqueous salt
a.	High	Green
b.	Low	Blue
c.	Medium	Pink
d.	High	Colorless

2. What happens when a piece of calcium chip is added to aqueous copper (II) sulphate?
    a. There will be a pink deposit of copper
    b. There will be a brown deposit of copper
    c. There will be a white ppt of calcium sulphate
    d. There will be a white ppt of copper calcide

3. Solution X contains ions of silver, potassium, calcium and lead. What happens when iron fillings are added to the solution?
    a. Only silver and lead will be displaced
    b. Only potassium and calcium will be displaced
    c. Only silver will be displaced
    d. Nothing will be displaced

4. Which metal can be obtained by heating its oxide with carbon?
    a. Calcium
    b. Sodium
    c. Silver
    d. Magnesium

5. Which metal can be obtained by heating its oxide in a stream of hydrogen gas?
    a. Copper
    b. Aluminium
    c. Calcium
    d. Zinc

6. Compound Z decomposes on heating to produce a black solid and a colourless gas. What is it?
   a. Copper (II) carbonate
   b. Sodium carbonate
   c. Lead carbonate
   d. Silver carbonate

7. 50g of iron fillings are added to a solution of copper (II) chloride. What could be the mass of iron fillings after the mixture is left to stand?
   a. 30g
   b. 50g
   c. 70g
   d. 100g

8. X and Y are both steels. X has a higher percentage of carbon than Y. What can be deduced?

	Stronger	More brittle
a.	X	Y
b.	X	X
c.	Y	Y
d.	Y	X

9. A piece of metal X that is stored with an iron block keeps the iron block from rusting. What is a possible identity of X?
   a. Zinc
   b. Copper
   c. Silver
   d. Lead

10. A piece of zinc is added to a mixture containing calcium carbonate and copper (II) chloride. What can be observed?
    a. A pink solid is deposited
    b. A gas that turns moist blue litmus paper red is liberated
    c. A gas that turns limewater chalky is liberated
    d. The solution turns green

11. Brass is an alloy. Which two metals are used to make brass?
    a. Copper, iron
    b. Iron, zinc
    c. Copper, zinc
    d. Copper, chromium

12. Why is brass harder than both the individual metals that are used to make it?
    a. The regular arrangement of the ions is disrupted
    b. A stronger compound is formed
    c. There are strong covalent bonds
    d. There are more electrons

13. Magnesium blocks are attached to a boat made of iron. What is the purpose of the magnesium blocks?
    a. To prevent the boat from rusting
    b. To make the boat stronger
    c. To prevent the boat from sinking
    d. To add colour to the boat

14. What is the name of the process described in the previous question
    a. Galvanization
    b. Sacrificial protection
    c. Painting
    d. Alloying

15. You are given the following information

Metal	Reaction with dilute HCl	Reaction with heated ZnO
A	Vigorous	Vigorous
B	Slow	None
C	None	None

What is the order of reactivity of metals A, B and C? In increasing order.

    a.   A, B, C
    b.   A, C, B
    c.   C, B, A
    d.   C, A, B

16. What happens to the oxidation state of metal A when it is added to a chloride salt of metal B?
    a.   Increases
    b.   Decreases
    c.   No change
    d.   Impossible to tell

17. What is the name of the process above?
    a.   Galvanization
    b.   Hydration
    c.   Alloying
    d.   Displacement

18. Molten cryolite is used in the extraction of aluminium from aluminium oxide. What is the main function of the molten cryolite?
    a.   Lower the melting point of the ore
    b.   Increase the melting point of the ore
    c.   Allow the ore to conduct electricity
    d.   Make the mixture more reactive

19. Name an element that has the following characteristics:

- Variable valency
- Can act as a catalyst
- Forms coloured compounds

a. Manganate
b. Bromine
c. Calcium
d. Aluminium

20. What is the special name given to the type of element above?
    a. Halogen
    b. Halide
    c. Transition metal
    d. Alkali metal

21. What happens when a piece of calcium chip is added to aqueous copper (II) sulphate?
    a. Calcium ions are oxidized
    b. Copper ions are oxidized
    c. Calcium ions are reduced
    d. Sulphate ions are reduced

22. Metal A reacts with cold water and steam. Metal B reacts with steam but not with cold water. Metal C reacts with neither cold water nor steam. List the metals in order of increasing reactivity.
    a. A, C, B
    b. A, B, C
    c. C, B, A
    d. C, A, B

23. Compare the products formed when metals A and B are reacted with steam. Name one similarity.
    a. Both are oxides
    b. Both are hydroxides
    c. Both are ionic
    d. Both are covalent

24. Compare the products formed when metals A and B are reacted with steam. Name one difference.
    a. One is a hydroxide, one is an oxide
    b. One is white, one is brown
    c. One can conduct electricity, the other cannot
    d. One is ionic, the other is covalent

25. What does not take place in a blast furnace?
    a. Oxidation of iron
    b. Reduction of carbon dioxide
    c. Oxidation of coke
    d. Oxidation of carbon monoxide

26. What happens when a piece of calcium chip is added to aqueous copper (II) sulphate?
    a. Calcium ions are oxidized
    b. Copper ions are oxidized
    c. Calcium atoms are oxidized
    d. Copper atoms are oxidized

27. Steel A has a higher percentage of carbon as compared to steel B. It is therefore…
    a. More malleable
    b. Coloured
    c. More brittle
    d. Weaker

28. Metal X reacts with steam but not cold water. Which is the most likely product when it is reacted with dilute sulphuric acid?
    a. Sodium sulphate
    b. Copper (II) sulphate
    c. Silver sulphate
    d. Zinc sulphate

29. Sacrificial protection is…
    a. When a less reactive metal is reacted in place of a more reactive metal
    b. When a more reactive metal is reacted in place of a less reactive metal
    c. When a less reactive metal is used to displace a more reactive metal
    d. When a more reactive metal is used to displace a less reactive metal

30. The extraction of iron from Haematite is a redox reaction. Why must the impurities be converted to slag?
    a. They are poisonous otherwise
    b. It is easier to remove
    c. So that more useful substances can be formed
    d. Slag can be sold for money

11 Electrolysis [__ / 30]

1. What is formed at the cathode?

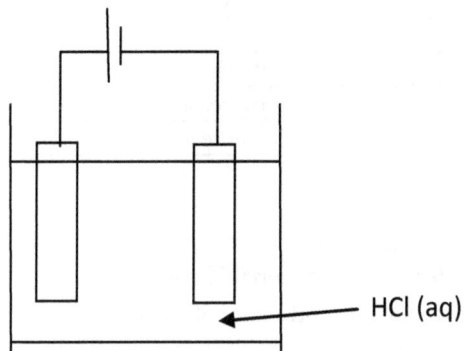

   a. Hydrogen gas
   b. Chlorine gas
   c. Oxygen gas
   d. Water

2. An electric current is passed through aqueous Potassium Nitrate with inert electrodes. What is formed at the anode?
   a. Hydrogen gas
   b. Potassium deposits
   c. Oxygen gas
   d. Nitrogen dioxide gas

3. In the electrolysis of liquid X using inert electrodes, the volume of the gas formed at the cathode is twice that of the gas formed at the anode. What could liquid X be?
   a. Aqueous copper (II) sulphate
   b. Concentrated HCl
   c. Molten NaCl
   d. Dilute H_2SO_4

4. In the electrolysis of Copper(II) Sulphate with Copper electrodes, how do the masses of the electrodes change?

	Mass of cathode	Mass of anode
a.	increases	Increases
b.	increases	Decreases
c.	decreases	Increases
d.	decreases	Decreases

5. In a simple cell using rods made of material X and material Y and dilute HCl as the electrolyte, bubbles are seen at the rod made of material Y. Which of the following must be true?
   a. X is more reactive than Y
   b. Y is more reactive than X
   c. There is no way to tell which material is more reactive
   d. X and Y are equally reactive

6. Molten NaCl is electrolysed using platinum electrodes. What is discharged at the cathode?
   a. Chlorine
   b. Hydrogen
   c. Oxygen
   d. Sodium

7. Concentrated potassium iodide is electrolysed using carbon electrodes. What is observed?

	cathode	Anode
a.	Bubbles are seen	Solution turns brown
b.	Bubbles are seen	Brown ppt deposited
c.	Solution turns brown	Solution turns dark purple
d.	Solution turns dark purple	Brown gas is liberated

8. Aqueous zinc chloride is electrolysed using platinum electrodes. What happens at the cathode?
   a. Zinc ions are oxidized
   b. Zinc ions are reduced
   c. Hydrogen ions are oxidized
   d. Hydrogen ions are reduced

9. What does not happen?

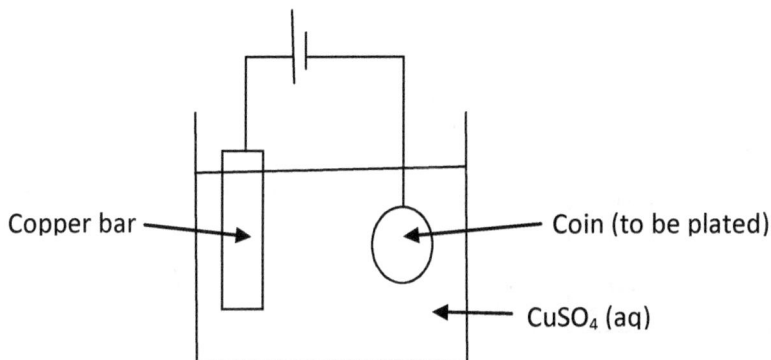

Copper bar → [electrode]   Coin (to be plated) → [electrode]   CuSO₄ (aq) →

a. Pink deposits form on the coin
b. The copper bar becomes smaller
c. The solution decolorizes
d. The coin becomes thicker

10. To electroplate a necklace with silver, what must be used as the anode?
   a. The necklace
   b. Carbon
   c. Platinum
   d. Silver

11. Concentrated aqueous lithium bromide is electrolysed with carbon electrodes. Which statement is true?
   a. Bromine gas forms at the cathode
   b. Oxygen gas forms at the anode
   c. Lithium deposits form at the cathode
   d. Hydrogen gas forms at the cathode

12. Which is responsible for conducting electricity in the wires in electrolysis?
   a. Mobile electrons
   b. Mobile ions
   c. Both mobile electrons and mobile ions
   d. Neither mobile electrons nor mobile ions

13. What could the experimental setup below possibly be?

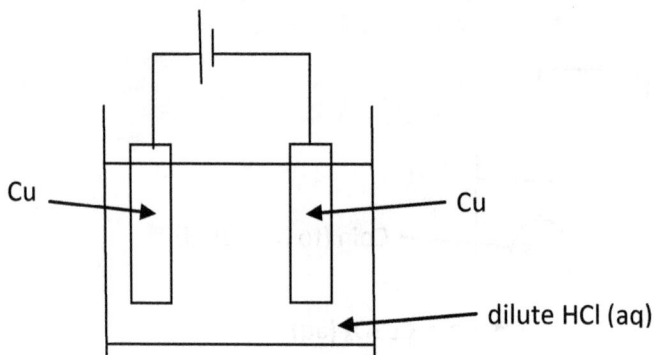

    a.   Electroplating
    b.   Purification
    c.   Galvanization
    d.   Sacrificial protection.

14. A simple cell is set up with dilute HCl as the electrolyte and electrodes made of aluminium and zinc. Which correctly describes the flow of electrons?
    a.   Through the wire, from the Al electrode to the Zn electrode
    b.   Through the wire, from the Zn electrode to the Al electrode
    c.   Through HCl (aq), from the Al electrode to the Zn electrode
    d.   Through HCl (aq), from the Zn electrode to the Al electrode

15. The highest current is required to discharge one mole of the following
    a.   Sodium
    b.   Zinc
    c.   Aluminium
    d.   Magnesium

16. What happens when concentrated NaCl (aq) is electrolysed using inert electrodes?
    a.   The pH of the solution increases
    b.   The pH of the solution decreases
    c.   There is no way to know how the pH of the solution changes
    d.   The pH of the solution is unaffected

17. Which requires the largest quantity of electricity in order to be discharged?
    a. 1 mole of aluminium ions
    b. 4 moles of zinc ions
    c. 6 moles of calcium ions
    d. 10 moles of potassium ions

18. An electrolytic cell has graphite electrodes and **dilute NaCl (aq)** as the electrolyte. Which statement is false?
    a. This is electrolysis of water
    b. Chlorine gas is given off at the anode
    c. Hydrogen gas is given off at the cathode
    d. The solution becomes more concentrated

19. Copper (II) sulfate is an electrolyte in an electrolytic cell with graphite electrodes. Which statement is true?
    a. The colour fades
    b. Copper is deposited at the anode
    c. Sulfur dioxide is given off at the anode
    d. Hydrogen gas is given off at the cathode

20. A simple cell is set up with

    i.   A voltmeter
    ii. An electrode made of Zinc
    iii. An electrode made of Lead
    iv. Dilute HCl as the electrolyte

What is observed?

    a. The lead electrode gets thinner
    b. The zinc electrode gets thinner
    c. Gas is evolved at the zinc electrode
    d. The solution turns white

21. What can be done to increase the reading on the voltmeter in the experiment above?
    a. Use iron in place of zinc
    b. Use iron in place of lead
    c. Use aluminium in place of zinc
    d. Use aluminium in place of lead

22. How would the results of the experiment be different if the same material is used for both electrodes?
    a. The voltmeter would show a slightly higher reading
    b. The voltmeter would show a slightly lower reading
    c. The voltmeter would show no reading
    d. It is voltmeter would spoil

23. At which electrode does oxidation occur?
    a. Zinc only
    b. Lead only
    c. Both electrodes
    d. None of the electrodes

24. The direction of electron flow in the wire is towards
    a. The left
    b. The right
    c. The top
    d. The bottom

25. Alcohol cannot be used as an electrolyte because it is
    a. Stable
    b. Reactive
    c. Not an electrical conductor
    d. Volatile

26. Which statement is true?
    a. Electrodes must be electrical conductors
    b. Electrolytes must be aqueous
    c. Electrolytes must be molten
    d. Electrodes must be metals

27. A simple cell is set up with zinc and metal X. The zinc electrode's mass decreases by 13g. What happens at metal X?
    a. Its mass increases by 13g
    b. Its mass also decreases by 13g
    c. 240 cm³ of hydrogen gas is released
    d. 480 cm³ of hydrogen gas is released

28. Which of the following statements must be true of two electrolytic cells joined in the same circuit when the mass of the deposits formed are different for each cell?
    a. The current flowing through is different
    b. Different electrolytes were used
    c. The one with a larger mass of deposits has more reactive metals as electrodes
    d. The one with a larger mass of deposits has less reactive metals as electrodes

29. What is electrolysis not used for?
    a. Extraction of metals
    b. Plating objects
    c. Purification
    d. Sacrificial protection

30. Choose the most accurate statement to describe a simple cell
    a. Neutralization always happens
    b. Reduction occurs at the more reactive electrode
    c. Oxidation occurs at the less reactive electrode
    d. All the statements above are inaccurate

12 Air [__ / 15]

1. The gas that is responsible for acid rain is
    a. Sulphur dioxide
    b. Carbon dioxide
    c. Carbon monoxide
    d. Methane

2. Which process is not part of the carbon cycle
    a. Respiration
    b. Photosynthesis
    c. Combustion
    d. Hydrogenation

3. Iron (II) ions in blood combine with which gas to prevent the blood from carrying oxygen?
    a. Nitrogen dioxide
    b. Carbon monoxide
    c. Carbon dioxide
    d. Sulphur trioxide

4. Which of the following substances, present in both air and car exhaust fumes, does not contribute to air pollution?
    a. Nitrogen
    b. Oxygen
    c. Nitrogen oxide
    d. Lead compounds

5. Which of the following is not found in car exhaust fumes?
    a. Water
    b. Oxygen
    c. Sulphur dioxide
    d. Nitrogen

6. Which statement is true concerning rusting, respiration and combustion?
   a. All produce carbon dioxide
   b. All are harmful to the environment
   c. All require oxygen
   d. All require sunlight

7. Limestone is another name for calcium carbonate. What happens when acid rain reacts with limestone?
   a. The pH of the acid rain increases
   b. The pH of the acid rain decreases
   c. Pungent gas is formed
   d. Oxygen is formed

8. Which is not a gas that leaves a catalytic converter?
   a. Nitrogen
   b. Carbon dioxide
   c. Carbon monoxide
   d. Steam

9. Ozone originates from
   a. Oxygen
   b. Noble gases
   c. Carbon dioxide
   d. Sulfur dioxide

10. Which is true?
   a. Ozone is never good for the atmosphere
   b. Ozone is never bad for the atmosphere
   c. Ozone is both good and bad for the atmosphere
   d. Ozone is neither good nor bad for the atmosphere

11. Which is responsible for the depletion of the ozone layer?
   a. Nitrogen dioxide
   b. Chlorine
   c. Fluorine
   d. Carbon monoxide

12. When the temperature of the water in a pond decreases, it is bad for the fish. Why?
    a. Oxygen is less soluble
    b. Harmful bacteria will grow
    c. They cannot reproduce
    d. The water becomes cloudy

13. Which is not present in dry air?
    a. Nitrogen
    b. Oxygen
    c. Argon
    d. Water vapour

14. Which is a source of nitrogen oxides?
    a. Lightning
    b. Rainwater
    c. Limestone buildings
    d. Photosynthesis

15. Which is not true of methane?
    a. It is a pollutant
    b. It is produced when cows chew grass
    c. It contributes to global warming
    d. It forms acid rain

13 Organic Chemistry [__ / 30]

1. Which must be true of hydrocarbons?
    a. They contain carbon atoms only
    b. They contain hydrogen atoms only
    c. They contain carbon and hydrogen atoms only
    d. They contain carbon, hydrogen and oxygen atoms only

2. Which must be true of all organic compounds?
    a. They contain carbon atoms
    b. They contain hydrogen atoms
    c. They contain oxygen atoms
    d. They contain nitrogen atoms

3. Pick the statement that is not true
    a. Crude oil is separated into its components by fractional distillation
    b. Flammability increases down the fractionating column
    c. Melting point increases down the fractionating column
    d. Viscosity increases down the fractionating column

4. Why is cracking important?
    a. To meet global demand for oil
    b. It is cheap
    c. It will save the environment
    d. Large hydrocarbon molecules are useless

5. What is used most often cracked to form petrol?
    a. Petroleum gas
    b. Naphtha
    c. Diesel
    d. Bitumen

6. Which of the following statements is true about solid fats and oil?
    a. Solid fats are saturated fat, oil is unsaturated
    b. Solid fats are unsaturated, oil is saturated
    c. Both solid fats and oil are saturated
    d. Both solid fats and oil are unsaturated

7. Which is a chemical test that can distinguish between vegetable oils and butter?
    a. Vegetable oils will turn limewater chalky
    b. Vegetable oils will delocolorize aqueous bromine solution
    c. Butter will turn red litmus paper blue
    d. Butter will form hydrogen bubbles with HCl

8. When a hydrocarbon undergoes complete combustion, what are the products formed?
    a. Carbon and hydrogen
    b. Carbon, hydrogen and oxygen
    c. Carbon dioxide, carbon monoxide and water
    d. Carbon dioxide and water

9. Which substance reacts with propane?
    a. Acidified potassium dichromate
    b. Ethanol
    c. Chlorine
    d. Water

10. Which physical property of alkenes increases with their relative molecular masses?
    a. Boiling point
    b. Electrical conductivity
    c. pH
    d. Reactivity

11. Why do alkanes not undergo addition reactions?
    a. They are unreactive
    b. They do not have C=C bonds
    c. Their boiling points are too high
    d. They do not have mobile ions or electrons

12. Which of the following compounds is most likely to be oxidized to a carboxylic acid?
    a. C_2H_6
    b. C_3H_8O
    c. HCOOH
    d. C_3H_6

13. How do isomers differ?
    a. They have different empirical formulas
    b. They have different chemical properties
    c. They have different structural formulas
    d. They have different pHs

14. Which of the following liberates a gas that forms a white ppt when bubbled through $Ca(OH)_2$?
    a. $CH_3COOC_2H_5$
    b. CH_3COOH
    c. C_2H_5OH
    d. C_2H_4

15. Which process requires a temperature of 300°C?
    a. Fermentation
    b. Esterification
    c. Hydration
    d. Cracking

16. In fermentation, an air lock is used. Why?
    a. To prevent carbon dioxide from entering
    b. To prevent the yeast from escaping
    c. To prevent the alcohol from escaping
    d. To prevent oxygen from entering

17. The products of fermentation are
    a. Glucose and ethanol
    b. Ethanol and water
    c. Ethanol and carbon dioxide
    d. Carbon dioxide and yeast

18. In the preparation of ethanol, hydration is preferred to fermentation. Why?
    a. Hydration does not require any catalyst
    b. Hydration is more efficient
    c. Fermentation is expensive
    d. Fermentation requires high temperature

19. Which substance can distinguish methanol from butane?
    a. Aqueous bromine
    b. Potassium dichromate
    c. Potassium iodide
    d. Hydrogen

20. Propanol can be manufactured by oxidizing
    a. Propane
    b. Propene
    c. Propanoic acid
    d. Propyl propanoate

21. How is ethanoic acid different from hydrochloric acid?
    a. It reacts with alcohols to form esters
    b. It reacts with copper to form a salt and hydrogen gas
    c. It neutralizes alkalis
    d. It reacts with metal carbonates to liberate carbon dioxide

22. Pentanoic acid
    a. Has 4 carbon atoms
    b. Is unsaturated
    c. Is saturated
    d. Has 6 carbon atoms

23. Which two reactants can be used to form butyl propanoate?
    a. Butane and propanol
    b. Butane and propanoic acid
    c. Butanol and propanoic acid
    d. Propanol and butanoic acid

24. What is the catalyst required in esterification?
    a. Dilute sulfuric acid
    b. Concentrated sulfuric acid
    c. Nickel
    d. Phosphoric acid

25. Esterification is
    a. Condensation polymerization
    b. Addition polymerization
    c. Halogenation
    d. Cracking

26. Suggest a commercial use for esters
    a. Making roads
    b. Fuel for cars
    c. Making perfumes
    d. Making lubricants

27. Name a similarity between nylon and terylene
    a. They are formed by addition polymerization
    b. They are formed by cracking
    c. They are formed by condensation polymerization
    d. They are formed by fermentation

28. Name a difference between nylon and terylene
    a. Nylon is soluble by terylene is not
    b. Nylon has an ester linkage but terylene has an amide linkage
    c. Nylon has an amide linkage but terylene has an ester linkage
    d. Nylon can conduct electricity but terylene cannot

29. Which has the same type of linkage as nylon?
    a. Fats
    b. Protein
    c. Poly(ethene)
    d. Petroleum

30. The combustion of organic compounds
    a. Can produce carbon monoxide
    b. Cannot produce carbon
    c. Is endothermic
    d. Requires a catalyst

9 781105 232824